The Pageant Journey

An Inspirational Journal Planner
for Cherishing the Journey & Preparing
for Your Success

Alicia "WATERS"

The Pageant Journey

Copyright © 2018 Alicia "WATERS"

All rights reserved. Except for use in the case of brief quotations embodied in critical articles and reviews, the reproduction or utilization of this work in whole or part in any form by any electronic, digital, mechanical or other means, now known or hereafter invented, including xerography, photocopying, scanning, recording, or any information storage or retrieval system, is forbidden without prior written permission of the author and publisher.

The scanning, uploading, and distribution of this book via the Internet or via any other means without permission of the publisher and author is illegal and punishable by law. Purchase only authorized versions of this book and do not participate in or encourage electronic piracy of copyrighted materials. Your support of the author's rights is appreciated.

Names, characters, places, and incidents are based on the author's own personal experience therefore names of persons and entities remain unnamed to protect the integrity of the story and the privacy of those involved. Any group or organization listed is for informational purposes only and does not imply endorsement or support of their activities or organization.
For ordering, booking, permission, or questions, contact the author.
www.anwempires@gmail.com

ISBN-13:978-1727445145

Printed in the United States of America by Create Space

The Pageant Journey

Cherishing the Pageant Journey
& Preparing for Your Success

"The journey is the reward." ~Steve Jobs

The adventures of the pageant industry can be exciting, challenging and/or turn out to be an audacious journey. This will be an experience that stays with you for a lifetime. You will discover that cherishing the journey along the way will keep you inspired to achieve your dreams. It's important every step along the way to prepare and plan for your success as best you can.

From the first to the last time that you walk across the stage, you will always be reminded that you've been a part of an epic experience that will help to open doors for many years to come.

Whether you're new to the pageant arena or have been competing for a while, you'll discover that it's important to continuously prepare and plan effectively. The time will fly by as you're having, fun, evolving into your best self or overcoming obstacles and setbacks.

It's vital to your success to stay focus and make sure that you plan an effective short, mid and long-term game plan for your success.

The Pageant Journey

Be sure to enroll the help of a mentor, pageant coach or others to get support. This will help to keep your commitment strong as you stay encouraged during the journey.

Every phase of your journey will require that you step up your game in certain areas as you make your mark in this industry.

The quality of experiences that you will have as a pageant contestant will be totally up to you. It's important to learn how to maximize and leverage your skills and the opportunities that come your way.

As mentioned previously, being in the pageant industry is a journey that should be cherished along the way. Use this journal planner to not only help you to plan your success but also as your sacred space to record your journey. You will create a life that is more than you can imagine on this journey.

The Pageant Journey

Cherishing the Pageant Journey
Creating My Success

Record your pageantry adventures and design your success.

The Pageant Journey

Cherishing the Pageant Journey
Creating My Success

Record your pageantry adventures and design your success.

The Pageant Journey

Cherishing the Pageant Journey
Creating My Success

Record your pageantry adventures and design your success.

The Pageant Journey

Cherishing the Pageant Journey
Creating My Success

Record your pageantry adventures and design your success.

The Pageant Journey

Cherishing the Pageant Journey
Creating My Success

Record your pageantry adventures and design your success.

The Pageant Journey

Cherishing the Pageant Journey
Creating My Success

Record your pageantry adventures and design your success.

The Pageant Journey

Cherishing the Pageant Journey
Creating My Success

Record your pageantry adventures and design your success.

The Pageant Journey

Cherishing the Pageant Journey
Creating My Success

Record your pageantry adventures and design your success.

The Pageant Journey

Cherishing the Pageant Journey
Creating My Success

Record your pageantry adventures and design your success.

The Pageant Journey

Cherishing the Pageant Journey
Creating My Success

Record your pageantry adventures and design your success.

The Pageant Journey

Cherishing the Pageant Journey
Creating My Success

Record your pageantry adventures and design your success.

The Pageant Journey

Cherishing the Pageant Journey
Creating My Success

Record your pageantry adventures and design your success.

The Pageant Journey

Cherishing the Pageant Journey Creating My Success

Record your pageantry adventures and design your success.

The Pageant Journey

Cherishing the Pageant Journey
Creating My Success

Record your pageantry adventures and design your success.

The Pageant Journey

Cherishing the Pageant Journey
Creating My Success

Record your pageantry adventures and design your success.

The Pageant Journey

Cherishing the Pageant Journey
Creating My Success

Record your pageantry adventures and design your success.

The Pageant Journey

Cherishing the Pageant Journey
Creating My Success

Record your pageantry adventures and design your success.

The Pageant Journey

Cherishing the Pageant Journey Creating My Success

Record your pageantry adventures and design your success.

The Pageant Journey

Cherishing the Pageant Journey
Creating My Success

Record your pageantry adventures and design your success.

The Pageant Journey

Cherishing the Pageant Journey
Creating My Success

Record your pageantry adventures and design your success.

The Pageant Journey

Cherishing the Pageant Journey
Creating My Success

Record your pageantry adventures and design your success.

The Pageant Journey

Cherishing the Pageant Journey
Creating My Success

Record your pageantry adventures and design your success.

The Pageant Journey

Cherishing the Pageant Journey
Creating My Success

Record your pageantry adventures and design your success.

The Pageant Journey

Cherishing the Pageant Journey
Creating My Success

Record your pageantry adventures and design your success.

The Pageant Journey

Cherishing the Pageant Journey
Creating My Success

Record your pageantry adventures and design your success.

The Pageant Journey

Cherishing the Pageant Journey
Creating My Success

Record your pageantry adventures and design your success.

The Pageant Journey

Cherishing the Pageant Journey
Creating My Success

Record your pageantry adventures and design your success.

The Pageant Journey

Cherishing the Pageant Journey
Creating My Success

Record your pageantry adventures and design your success.

The Pageant Journey

Cherishing the Pageant Journey
Creating My Success

Record your pageantry adventures and design your success.

The Pageant Journey

Cherishing the Pageant Journey
Creating My Success

Record your pageantry adventures and design your success.

The Pageant Journey

Cherishing the Pageant Journey
Creating My Success

Record your pageantry adventures and design your success.

The Pageant Journey

Cherishing the Pageant Journey
Creating My Success

Record your pageantry adventures and design your success.

The Pageant Journey

Cherishing the Pageant Journey
Creating My Success

Record your pageantry adventures and design your success.

The Pageant Journey

Cherishing the Pageant Journey
Creating My Success

Record your pageantry adventures and design your success.

The Pageant Journey

Cherishing the Pageant Journey
Creating My Success

Record your pageantry adventures and design your success.

The Pageant Journey

Cherishing the Pageant Journey
Creating My Success

Record your pageantry adventures and design your success.

The Pageant Journey

Cherishing the Pageant Journey
Creating My Success

Record your pageantry adventures and design your success.

The Pageant Journey

Cherishing the Pageant Journey
Creating My Success

Record your pageantry adventures and design your success.

The Pageant Journey

Cherishing the Pageant Journey
Creating My Success

Record your pageantry adventures and design your success.

The Pageant Journey

Cherishing the Pageant Journey
Creating My Success

Record your pageantry adventures and design your success.

The Pageant Journey

Cherishing the Pageant Journey
Creating My Success

Record your pageantry adventures and design your success.

The Pageant Journey

Cherishing the Pageant Journey
Creating My Success

Record your pageantry adventures and design your success.

The Pageant Journey

Cherishing the Pageant Journey
Creating My Success

Record your pageantry adventures and design your success.

The Pageant Journey

Cherishing the Pageant Journey
Creating My Success

Record your pageantry adventures and design your success.

The Pageant Journey

Cherishing the Pageant Journey
Creating My Success

Record your pageantry adventures and design your success.

The Pageant Journey

Cherishing the Pageant Journey
Creating My Success

Record your pageantry adventures and design your success.

The Pageant Journey

Cherishing the Pageant Journey
Creating My Success

Record your pageantry adventures and design your success.

The Pageant Journey

Cherishing the Pageant Journey
Creating My Success

Record your pageantry adventures and design your success.

The Pageant Journey

Cherishing the Pageant Journey
Creating My Success

Record your pageantry adventures and design your success.

The Pageant Journey

Cherishing the Pageant Journey
Creating My Success

Record your pageantry adventures and design your success.

The Pageant Journey

Cherishing the Pageant Journey
Creating My Success

Record your pageantry adventures and design your success.

The Pageant Journey

Cherishing the Pageant Journey
Creating My Success

Record your pageantry adventures and design your success.

The Pageant Journey

Cherishing the Pageant Journey
Creating My Success

Record your pageantry adventures and design your success.

The Pageant Journey

Cherishing the Pageant Journey
Creating My Success

Record your pageantry adventures and design your success.

The Pageant Journey

Cherishing the Pageant Journey
Creating My Success

Record your pageantry adventures and design your success.

The Pageant Journey

Cherishing the Pageant Journey
Creating My Success

Record your pageantry adventures and design your success.

The Pageant Journey

Cherishing the Pageant Journey
Creating My Success

Record your pageantry adventures and design your success.

The Pageant Journey

Cherishing the Pageant Journey
Creating My Success

Record your pageantry adventures and design your success.

The Pageant Journey

Cherishing the Pageant Journey
Creating My Success

Record your pageantry adventures and design your success.

The Pageant Journey

Cherishing the Pageant Journey
Creating My Success

Record your pageantry adventures and design your success.

The Pageant Journey

Cherishing the Pageant Journey
Creating My Success

Record your pageantry adventures and design your success.

The Pageant Journey

Cherishing the Pageant Journey
Creating My Success

Record your pageantry adventures and design your success.

The Pageant Journey

Cherishing the Pageant Journey
Creating My Success

Record your pageantry adventures and design your success.

The Pageant Journey

Cherishing the Pageant Journey
Creating My Success

Record your pageantry adventures and design your success.

The Pageant Journey

Cherishing the Pageant Journey
Creating My Success

Record your pageantry adventures and design your success.

The Pageant Journey

Cherishing the Pageant Journey
Creating My Success

Record your pageantry adventures and design your success.

The Pageant Journey

Cherishing the Pageant Journey
Creating My Success

Record your pageantry adventures and design your success.

The Pageant Journey

Cherishing the Pageant Journey
Creating My Success

Record your pageantry adventures and design your success.

The Pageant Journey

Cherishing the Pageant Journey
Creating My Success

Record your pageantry adventures and design your success.

The Pageant Journey

Cherishing the Pageant Journey
Creating My Success

Record your pageantry adventures and design your success.

The Pageant Journey

Cherishing the Pageant Journey
Creating My Success

Record your pageantry adventures and design your success.

The Pageant Journey

Cherishing the Pageant Journey
Creating My Success

Record your pageantry adventures and design your success.

The Pageant Journey

Cherishing the Pageant Journey
Creating My Success

Record your pageantry adventures and design your success.

The Pageant Journey

Cherishing the Pageant Journey
Creating My Success

Record your pageantry adventures and design your success.

The Pageant Journey

Cherishing the Pageant Journey
Creating My Success

Record your pageantry adventures and design your success.

The Pageant Journey

Cherishing the Pageant Journey
Creating My Success

Record your pageantry adventures and design your success.

The Pageant Journey

Cherishing the Pageant Journey
Creating My Success

Record your pageantry adventures and design your success.

The Pageant Journey

Cherishing the Pageant Journey
Creating My Success

Record your pageantry adventures and design your success.

The Pageant Journey

Cherishing the Pageant Journey
Creating My Success

Record your pageantry adventures and design your success.

The Pageant Journey

Cherishing the Pageant Journey
Creating My Success

Record your pageantry adventures and design your success.

The Pageant Journey

Cherishing the Pageant Journey
Creating My Success

Record your pageantry adventures and design your success.

The Pageant Journey

Cherishing the Pageant Journey
Creating My Success

Record your pageantry adventures and design your success.

The Pageant Journey

Cherishing the Pageant Journey
Creating My Success

Record your pageantry adventures and design your success.

The Pageant Journey

Cherishing the Pageant Journey
Creating My Success

Record your pageantry adventures and design your success.

The Pageant Journey

Cherishing the Pageant Journey
Creating My Success

Record your pageantry adventures and design your success.

The Pageant Journey

Cherishing the Pageant Journey
Creating My Success

Record your pageantry adventures and design your success.

The Pageant Journey

Cherishing the Pageant Journey
Creating My Success

Record your pageantry adventures and design your success.

The Pageant Journey

Cherishing the Pageant Journey
Creating My Success

Record your pageantry adventures and design your success.

The Pageant Journey

Cherishing the Pageant Journey
Creating My Success

Record your pageantry adventures and design your success.

The Pageant Journey

Cherishing the Pageant Journey
Creating My Success

Record your pageantry adventures and design your success.

The Pageant Journey

Cherishing the Pageant Journey
Creating My Success

Record your pageantry adventures and design your success.

The Pageant Journey

Cherishing the Pageant Journey
Creating My Success

Record your pageantry adventures and design your success.

The Pageant Journey

Cherishing the Pageant Journey
Creating My Success

Record your pageantry adventures and design your success.

The Pageant Journey

Cherishing the Pageant Journey
Creating My Success

Record your pageantry adventures and design your success.

The Pageant Journey

Cherishing the Pageant Journey
Creating My Success

Record your pageantry adventures and design your success.

The Pageant Journey

For More Resources:
Visit:
www.thepageantjourney.tumblr.com
www.amazon.com/author/alicianwaters

To Book Author
for Speaking Engagements
Email:
www.anwempires@gmail.com

The Pageant Journey

Made in the USA
Coppell, TX
14 February 2020